Althea (

Pioneer of the Tennis Courts

by Barbara A. Donovan

Harcourt
SCHOOL PUBLISHERS

Cover, Bettmann/CORBIS; 3, AP Photo/John Lent; 4, Bettmann/CORBIS; 5, Ralph Morse/Time Life Pictures/Getty Images; 6, 7, 8, Bettmann/CORBIS; 10, Andre Jenny/Alamy; 11, Bert Hardy/Picture Post/Getty Images; 12, AFP/Getty Images; 13, Bettmann/CORBIS; 14, AP Photo.

Printed in the United States of America

ISBN 10: 0-15-351686-0
ISBN 13: 978-0-15-351686-3

Ordering Options
ISBN 10: 0-15-351216-4 (Grade 6 Advanced Collection)
ISBN 13: 978-0-15-351216-2 (Grade 6 Advanced Collection)
ISBN 10: 0-15-358169-7 (package of 5)
ISBN 13: 978-0-15-358169-4 (package of 5)

1 2 3 4 5 6 7 8 9 10 179 12 11 10 09 08 07 06

Growing Up in Harlem

Althea Gibson didn't fit into anyone's mold. She wasn't a good student. She wasn't a dainty little girl. Instead, she loved to play football and other sports. Fortunately, someone noticed her gift for tennis at an early age. She'd need great talent to propel her to the top of her sport. To reach the top, she would also need to break the sport's color barrier because she was an African American. At the time, African Americans were not welcome to compete against white people in most sports leagues.

Born on August 25, 1927, in South Carolina, Althea and her family moved to Harlem in New York City when she was only three. Althea liked city life and was always getting into some kind of mischief. There seemed to be no remedies for her misbehaving.

For Althea, school was a struggle. She was too interested in her friends and sports to settle down to schoolwork. She intensely disliked everything about school.

When Althea was a young teen, she dropped out of school. However, her natural ability as an athlete was about to turn her life around. At the time, the Police Athletic League (PAL) of New York had a street play program. During the day, certain streets in each neighborhood were blocked off so that the kids who lived there could have a safe place to play. PAL sponsored many sports, including paddle tennis. Althea was a natural at this game. Her height of 5 feet 11 inches (about 1.5 m) helped her when she lunged for the ball. It didn't take her long to become the champion of her block.

Buddy Walker was a musician who worked summers as a play leader for PAL. As he watched Althea play paddle tennis, he had an idea. He bought two tennis rackets and began practicing with her. He realized right away that Althea could be a tennis star.

Buddy Walker brought Althea to some nearby tennis courts. Her play that first day filled other players with astonishment. One of the men watching thought that Althea should play at the Cosmopolitan Tennis Club. For Althea, this was an honor because the club was a private tennis club.

Althea was eager to play at the Cosmopolitan. Before long, she was set to play against the club's professional, Fred Johnson. Althea's play against Johnson was so strong that some members chipped in so that she could become a junior member. Now she could take lessons from Mr. Johnson and learn about her sport. She learned footwork and how to place the ball where she wanted it.

Althea's coach, Fred Johnson

In 1942, one year after her first tennis lesson, Althea was ready for her first tournament. The Cosmopolitan Club was hosting the New York State Open Championship for the American Tennis Association (ATA). The ATA was a tennis organization with a mostly African American membership, so Althea playing in this tournament was not a problem. Her event was girls' singles. She beat every player she played against. She ended the tournament as its triumphant winner.

Later that same summer, Althea reached the final match in the ATA National Championship but lost against Nana Davis. The following year, the ATA National Championship was cancelled. World War II had limited travel from city to city. When the championship started again, in 1944 and 1945, Althea won the top spot. She had become the girls' singles champion.

Getting Into Focus

The year 1945 was a turning point in Althea's life. Turning eighteen made her eligible for the ATA national women's title in 1946. She would be facing the best and most experienced women in the ATA. Once again, Althea beat player after player. At last, she reached the finals, but she was overconfident and believed that she'd win easily. Instead, her opponent returned each of Althea's shots and won the match. Althea had fumbled her chance for the championship, but she had learned an important lesson—never underestimate your opponent.

Althea may have lost the women's title, but her play had been impressive. It was so strong that Dr. Hubert A. Eaton and Dr. Robert W. Johnson made a surprising proposal. They wanted Althea to move to Wilmington, North Carolina, and complete her high school education there. She'd live with Dr. Eaton's family during the school year and play tennis on his courts. Then she'd move in with Dr. Johnson's family in Lynchburg, Virginia, each summer. There she would get more lessons and play in many tournaments.

As generous and thrilling as the offer was, Althea was concerned about the move. She was a city girl. She knew what to expect and how to take care of herself in Harlem, but not in the South, where she knew life would be different for her as an African American.

Althea was prepared to turn the offer down when her friends, Sugar Ray Robinson, the famous boxer, and his wife, convinced her that this was the offer of a lifetime. They told her that this was her chance to get an education. It was a chance to make something of herself. In September 1946, Althea arrived in Wilmington to start the tenth grade.

When Althea arrived at Dr. Eaton's home, she was accepted as if she'd always belonged there. Althea had never experienced such luxury. She was determined to make the most of her fresh start.

For Althea, life in the South was not nearly as horrible as she had imagined. Still, the unfairness of how African Americans were treated by many stung her. Life in the Eaton house was good, but life for an African American in the South was difficult.

In addition to her schoolwork, Althea played tennis with Dr. Eaton on his private courts. During vacation, she moved in with Dr. Johnson's family so that she could practice her game all summer. Day by day, Althea improved. By the end of the summer of 1947, she'd won the singles championship in all nine tournaments she'd entered. That included the ATA National Championship against none other than Nana Davis, her former opponent. Together with Dr. Johnson, she'd won eight mixed doubles championships. No one could doubt it now—Althea Gibson was the best player in the ATA. No one could beat her. In fact, no one did beat her in the ATA National Championships for ten years in a row.

Althea thanks her friend Sugar Ray Robinson

By 1949, Dr. Eaton and Dr. Johnson were certain that it was time for Althea to take a giant leap in the world of tennis. When Dr. Eaton asked Althea if she was ready to play at Forest Hills, she knew exactly what he was really asking. Was she ready to play for the championship of the all-white United States Lawn Tennis Association (USTLA)? Yes, Althea was ready.

The first step was to enter Althea in the Eastern Indoor Championship, which was to be played in New York City. She played fairly well but lost in the quarterfinals. She was the only African American woman in the tournament, and the other women treated her as well and as politely as she had come to expect from tennis players. Althea stayed in the city for another tournament. This time she'd be the first African American woman to play for the National Indoor Championship. Though she didn't win, it was still a great accomplishment.

Althea had done a lot of growing up in those three years. In June of 1949, she graduated from high school. She applied and was accepted to Florida A&M University in Tallahassee, which also offered her a tennis scholarship. The coach wanted her in Florida, practicing her tennis that summer, so Althea packed her bags, bid the Eatons good-bye, and left for college.

Becoming Somebody

Althea's college life was full of tennis practice and tournaments, studying, and working to earn spending money. She was invited to the National Indoor Championships again in 1950, but she lost in the finals. Althea felt proud of how far she had come and knew she would keep knocking at the door to the championship until she won it. When she arrived back in Tallahassee after her defeat, she was met at the train station by the college band and many supporters. Even though she'd lost the tournament, she knew that getting to the finals was a point of pride for other African Americans.

Althea's good showing at the National Indoor Championship caused her to get a flood of invitations to play in major tournaments. If she played well in these important matches, the USLTA would have to invite her to play at Forest Hills. Even though she didn't win these tournaments, she played well enough for one of the USLTA officials to say that if she applied for the National Championship in Forest Hills, she'd be accepted.

Then, after she had applied, the USLTA dragged its feet. Weeks went by with no word. Finally, one tennis champion, Alice Marble, wrote a letter to the editor of a tennis magazine. In it, she wrote that Althea Gibson had earned the right to play at Forest Hills. Excluding her because she was an African American was not admirable of them.

In the middle of August 1950, Althea was invited to play at the nationals in Forest Hills, New York. She didn't win, but it was a historic moment. It was the first time an African American woman had played in this important tournament. Over the next three years, Althea finished college and played in many tournaments, including Wimbledon in England, but she was never able to win there.

By the time she finished college in 1955, Althea was set to give up on tennis until she was asked if she'd like to go on a goodwill tour for the State Department of the United States. She accepted the offer right away. Althea and three other American tennis players traveled to different countries where they played tennis, answered questions, and feasted on local foods. The trip was a huge success for the State Department and for Althea herself. She won sixteen of the eighteen tournaments she played while on the trip.

Queen Elizabeth II of England congratulates Althea at Wimbledon

In 1956, Althea was the champion in tournaments in France, Italy, and Asia. However, wins at prestigious Forest Hills and Wimbledon were still only a dream for her. In 1957, Althea returned to Wimbledon in England. One by one, she beat her opponents and reached the final match. The Queen of England was in the stands watching her play, and she would hand the trophy to the winner. With all her stamina and determination, Althea won the match! She was the first African American champion of Wimbledon!

Althea's feat was sensational news. There was a parade for her in New York City. The mayor gave her a medal. However, she still had one more hurdle to jump—Forest Hills.

As with Wimbledon in 1957, Althea reached the finals at Forest Hills and won. She was the first African American USTLA National Champion. Then to prove that her wins were not just flukes, she went back and won at both Wimbledon and Forest Hills again the next year.

In 1957 and 1958, Althea was voted Female Athlete of the Year. She continued to play tennis, and when she was older, she taught the sport to others. She even took up golf, though tennis was the sport she excelled in. In 1975, she became New Jersey State Commissioner of Athletics, a position she held for ten years.

Althea died on September 28, 2003, at the age of seventy-six. She continues to inspire people to this day. Tennis legend Billie Jean King said Althea helped to pave the way for other tennis champions.

Think Critically

1. List in chronological order the key accomplishments in Althea Gibson's tennis career.

2. How did tennis change Althea Gibson's life?

3. If you could ask Althea Gibson what the most important event in her life was, what do you think her answer would be?

4. Why does the title of this book call Althea Gibson a pioneer of the tennis courts?

5. What do you admire most about Althea Gibson?

Social Studies

Write Interview Questions Imagine that you are going to interview Althea Gibson. What questions would you like to ask her? Write the questions and think about how she might have answered them.

School-Home Connection Explain to your family who Althea Gibson was and how she changed the face of tennis. Then try to think of other people who have broken barriers in sports and other fields.

Word Count: 1,997